I adore Richard Loranger' out into the world, spotlighting our connection/disconnection with the earth and our highest selves. Be it celebrating nature or exposing the malice of MAGA America, Loranger places the human condition under the poetic microscope and grapples with how to make peace with our alternately magic and savage selves. He not only reveals a world where we are stuck between home and hard places—such as sorrow, jealousy, and racism—but also shows us how poetry can transform strife and oppression into a healing lyrical medicine.

- Rich Ferguson, State of CA Beat Poet Laureate (as selected by the National Beat Poetry Foundation, 2020-2022)

Richard Loranger is a wry and inventive poet with a deft touch. His collection *Unit of Agency* proves him a language alchemist revitalizing words and infusing them with blistering new energy. "I don't know what any of this means," he writes. "Because this isn't about meaning. It's about being. It's about doing. It's about living."

- James Cagney, author of *Black Steel Magnolias in The Hour of Chaos Theory*, winner of the PEN Oakland 2019 Josephine Miles Award

Richard Loranger's poetry is an exhilarating and dizzying bouillabaisse of seminal psychosexual seriousness and silliness. He is optimally prime in his moment to moment transformation, construction and deconstruction of what we might be, what we could and what we is. *Unit of Agency* is a new pocket universe on every read and I look forward to every trip back.

- Juba Kalamka, author of *Son of Byford,* member of "homohop" group Rainbow Flava, co-founder/producer of Deep Dickollective (D/DC), and developer of the micro-label Sugartruck Recordings

UNIT OF AGENCY

Richard Loranger

‾.... . ‾.‾. . .‾ ..‾ .... .

.‾‾ .

Introduction by Lonely Christopher

COLLAPSE
PRESS

This book is the inaugural publication by

COLLAPSE PRESS

www.collapsepress.com

Copyright © 2021 Richard Loranger

All Rights Reserved

ISBN: 978-1-7352669-1-6

Cover image: "Warden's House on Alcatraz Island"

Cover design by E. Lynn Alexander

Cover photo by Richard Loranger, 2016

Bio photo by Leigh Loranger, 1990

Back cover photo by Jane Ormerod, 2018

Author's website: www.richardloranger.com

Author's contact: hello@richardloranger.com

AUTHOR'S NOTE ON REPRODUCTION

The texts in this book frequently make clear that the author is not at all fond of the excesses and destructive nature of Late Capitalist culture. He does, however, believe that the burgeoning yet struggling industry of independent presses is integral in opposing those excesses and the dissemination of ideas that could to some extent mitigate that destruction while it ensues. If you should copy a few pages from this book for use in a classroom or workshop, as is commonly done, he asks that you credit him as the writer, the book's title, and the publisher, Collapse Press, on each piece. He also encourages you to support this and all small presses by purchasing their publications whenever you are able, and he hopes that you will encourage others to do the same. Finally, he hopes that you will enjoy reading the pieces in this book as much as he enjoyed writing them.

For those who we

TABLE OF CONTENTS

Introduction

Richard Loranger is a busy mammal of motley experience. Not in this order: he's been a queer punk activist and provocateur; an officiator of weddings; a visual artist whose work has been exhibited more than a dozen times; a founding member of the storied Babar Poets community; a member of the Bay Area rock band Baldo Rex in the late 80s; a performance artist as part of San Francisco's High Risk Group; a baritone in an *a capella* choir named Conspiracy of Beards, which covers Leonard Cohen songs; a professor at Brooklyn College, City College, Pratt Institute, and Rutgers University; a bicoastal editor of little magazines; a fervent blogger; a creative consultant...the list goes on. He is highly anthologized and the author of ten chapbooks, including the notorious *The Day Was Warm and Blue* and *Hello Poems*, a pocket-sized dialogue piece that serves as his calling card. His first full-length poetry collection, *The Orange Book*, was published in 1990, followed some years later by *Poems for Teeth* in 2005, which uses the angst of extensive dental problems as a generative technique, naming all of his teeth and expounding upon their magical purposes. There is an ongoing tension between order and chaos in that work, as if methodical thinking might open up into a deeper wildness.

Ever eclectically minded, Loranger's creative projects evince an expanding variety of genre, tone, voice, and style. He's been lumped in with such disparate practices as neoformalism, punk rock, and performance art, and parts of his corpus align compellingly with one mode of expression or another, but Loranger is braver and more exploratory than many of his contemporaries, willing (enthusiastic, really) to take risks and follow fancies. His techniques are peripatetic and yet his authorial voice is strong and identifiable. Following turning his mouth into a menagerie of pain and hope in the verse forms of *Teeth*, he published a meditative jangle of flash prose titled *Sudden Windows* in 2015, then a mixture of formal attacks in last year's uplifting chapbook *Be a Bough Tit*, its sense of play evident from the title's homophonic reimagining of the name of its publisher, Be About It Press. I happen to know he's recently finished a novel—the innovation continues!

Often there's a sense of celebration present in Loranger's work, a joyous alternative to the bleak, angry, and pessimistic sociopolitical atmosphere we've endured as virulent media throbs under burning skies. This isn't masochism, it's a form of alchemy, spinning shit into gold, finding a light, meeting the worst and giving it your best. In the interest of existence, he finds, at a certain point one must insist: "Fuck the ideologies. Let's have a world." While Loranger's work brims with such anarchoradicality, he's also (or should I say "therefore"?) interested in establishing an ethics of care.

Which brings us to this book. *Unit of Agency* could only have followed the Trump administration, when the last shreds of U.S. democracy were forced to the brink. Luckily, this is not Richard Loranger's first ride on the merry-go-round. His long history of oppositional defiance provides much ammunition against encroaching political catastrophe. Loranger's known the score for years—that the big machine was falling apart but the bosses were going to drive it into the ground. He's finely attuned to the brand of lethal hypocrisy that's invaded our discourse. He'll tell you, in fact, that nothing's new under the sun. This shit has always been going on. It's just that the sun's getting hotter and the world grows weary and weird. The extreme ravages of the Covid pandemic were much less surprising to those who survived the Plague Years of AIDS firsthand and intimately understood the government's depthless apathy and cruelty. Problems of community and sustainability are beside the imperative for consumption—and no longer must proponents of the capitalistic death cult pretend otherwise.

Richard Loranger's poetry embraces the mammalian condition in all its contradictions, dangers, and beauty. Despite the rampant sublimity of his verse, it's implicitly political. The imploration that "we have to become human" recognizes a moral imperative for resistance, actively confronting a sociopolitical infrastructure explicitly designed to alienate us from our communities and ultimately ourselves, detach us from our responsibilities, become consumerist screens, dissociatively labile. Loranger prescribes no concrete answers but architects ramshackle systems of thought through which to jostle and unhorse our indolent prejudices, reach out for something more, find the materials to start building. Loranger declares that eroding forces "can oppress but they cannot destroy," leaving room for a flickering survival that might foment revolution. He situates the fulcrum of radical potentiality in group consciousness, or at the very least recognition, cooperation. The poem "#we" is pebbled with the first-person singular pronoun "I," showing how the individual may be realized through the communal. Welcoming the we is to "wake up" to "the verb of we" in an act of allowance and acceptance. Active reception requires vulnerability, but that's the risk taken to "nourish from the milk of each other's hearts." A possibly maudlin and surely messy proposition to empower "the kaleidoscopic whorl of being."

Loranger spars brutally with fascist politics in his series of "MAGA Poems" ("Make America Great Again" being the acronymic slogan for Trumpism), mocking the economy's insupportable appetites by appropriating the toxic rhetoric of neoconservative pundits who now proudly admit the endgame: "make as much money as possible,/as fast as possible,/by doing as little as possible." During the Trump administration, we were inundated with the executive's childish and cruel language on a daily basis for years. It was inescapable, assaultive. His simplistic hatefulness encouraged racist goons to quack openly in torch-carrying hordes about how "the Jews will not replace us," or run over leftist activists in their cars, or attack women and People of Color generally and constantly. The poet deploys sarcasm and irony with an enraged acuity exacerbated by the cartoonish bombast of bootlicking chauvinists. The flag-waving speaker of Loranger's MAGA series becomes increasingly unhinged and senseless, until his defense of "freedom" degrades into threats: "Fuck you go die." In those four words Loranger has distilled the essence of the modern political consciousness. Liberty from existence—the ultimate win. A reader may bristle at the procession of borrowed nationalist invective, although the poet provides us with the required catharsis by having this character accidentally kill himself while demonstrating to his victim how they should eat a gun. That implicates the self-devouring nature of supremacy ideology.

Late capitalism consumes so much energy but generates no light, only heat. A leader that cares about their nation is a Whitmanesque fantasy. Corporations are both immortal and granted legal rights of personhood. Bureaucratic systems of service provision are suffused in the language of surveillance. Capitalism is "eating itself from the inside" without the awareness that, like a virus, it is destroying its host. Amidst this dangerous circus, the poet is "daggered and sliced" by an absurd reality but remains undefeated. Perhaps these poems find Loranger at his most cynical, yet he can't surrender the drive for healing. There's something unredeemable about the human condition that must be met with rage but also grace. Writing under the calcine skies of a "broken city," Loranger strikes the balance.

Lonely Christopher
August 2021

UNIT OF AGENCY

DIY

Here's a leaf.
Take a piece of your mind and put it on a plate.
Here's a hammer.
Take a piece of your mind and slam it on the table.
Here's a brick.
Take a piece of your mind and let me hear it, let me hear it.
Let me take it home and coddle it and fight with it and feed it a
    good meal.
Let me smell it and touch it and find the parts I know.
Here's the sky.
Here's a knot.
Here's a cinch.
Take a piece of your mind and slap me.
Throw it in the street.
Let it run loose. Let it scream a bit.
Take a piece of you and, I'm telling you, you're gonna live, you're
    gonna die, what's it worth, put your hand on the block and
    strike. Goddamn it. What do you want? You wanna live?
Here's a fly. Here's a plane. Here're two pieces of wood. A
    basket. A shotgun. A piece of fruit.
Here's the law.
Take your fuckin mind and charge it, slam it, sear it through, fling
    it at the world. What culture? What celebration?
    Gluttonous dogs. Renders of meat. Capsules.
Here's my hand.
Take your mind and do what you want with it. What do you want
    to do? Chant on? Multiply? Strike the dogs down? Eat
    sand? Recant? Defend your property? Extend your hand?
    Stab me quickly? Kick back and live it, live it up, live it all
    the way, fuck it, spew, cover the land in mounds of fat, rank
    spores, morbid scree?
Capsules. Polyps. Is that what you are?
Here's your mind.
Take it. It's yours. It's all yours, what is yours, what chunk is
    yours, is this your life? Fling it. Strike the dogs. It's yours.
    For how long? What do you want?
Here's a leaf. Goddamn it, a leaf.

1

Here's culture. Once a celebration. Once tidings. Once gratitude and grace.
Here's a hammer.

WE HAVE TO BECOME HUMAN

We have to become human if we want to be pumas.
We have to become human if we want to be Schubert.
We have to become human if we want to be truthful.
We have to become human if we want a big choo-choo.
We have to become human if we want to eat rhubarb.
We have to become human if we want to ruminate.
We have to become human if we want to hear roosters.
We have to become human if we want a blue frou-frou.
We have to become human if we want to speak Zulu.
We have to become human if we want to wear bloomers.
We have to become human if we want a pluperfect.
We have to become human if we want to shoo-be-doo-be-doo.
We have to become human if we want to see Newton.
We have to become human if we want to push broomsticks.
We have to become human if we want to seek sutras.
We have to become human if we want to meet Rumi.
We have to become human if we want to free Mumia.
We have to become human if we want to be ruthful.
We have to become human if we want to drink root beer.
We have to become human if we don't want a boo-boo.
We have to become human if we don't want in lieu of.
We have to become human if we want a new room.

remember:

delivered well + orderly we
rip our skin off rip our
rip our skin + shine like the bloody
moon the moon that pulls us
out of the room the room that
held us tight like skin. rip
the moon you well-delivered orderly you
roustabout rousted from sleep by the shining
police uttering words made of skin.
the police uttering nonsense uttering death
are sent by the carnival balloons the
unspent corporations muttering hoc est corpus
hoc est corpus the police muttering nonsense
muttering other. the other police are not so bad
are not sent or crooned only
crowd the balustrade when justice intervenes.
the ballooned corporation edges tensely toward
the body, the corpus hailed and reigned
in an orderly delivery. the corpus, the corporation, the police
deliver well the taut balloon but cannot
pinch the moon, cannot pull us uttering + bloody
from the unorderly carnival the unspent shine
because we are not held in by skin,
because we are beyond skin we are
ripped we are bloody + blooded + well,
because we are sinew + nerve + eyes + they cannot destroy eyes,
they can oppress but they cannot destroy
because eyes see + eyes speak + eyes listen + sinew resists
because they cannot live without our eyes
because they need our eyes to see
because without being seen they are nothing
because without us they are nothing
because they are already nothing
because we see that
because we are eyes
because we are blood

because we are blood and mind
because we.

THE OAKLAND SKY

cracks like a smartphone screen
splintering grey and orange-red pulsing
with the blood of the dispossessed.
The streets run rivers of ions
pixelating between lo and hi def
def problematic for the common man
still trying to buy lettuce at the corner store.
There is nothing common about this town
once pounding with jazz and ships and strife
now mesmerized by the bullshit addiction
staring us in the face all day long.
We stare at selfies while the colonists yelp
and foam about us like the tidal scum
lapping at the dying docks and the refabbed clubs
that charge a dollar for a nickel's worth.
What is a dollar to a prince of light?
The true folk dwell in shadows as the towers loom,
stripped of their sky and yanked from their birth rooms
by the googooing hand of cash that can't
tell a good man from a mad dog's grin.
The hounds are upon us, as they've been before,
West Bay lost already to the puke of lords,
as we stand along this ancient shore fending
kindness and culture and histories and lives
from the throats and jaws of the rising tide
that surges howling *my sky, my sky* like an idiot mutt
ripped from its brood and plopped in a new backyard.
The Oakland sky belongs to Oakland, nothing more,
and what Oakland is is culled from hills
and streams and sediment, sandstone, basalt, quartz, and shale,
roots of live oak, bay tree, lavender, blackberry, and flowering sage,
hummingbirds and hawks, wild turkey, cormorants, jays, and crow,
coyotes, gray fox, brush rabbit, bobcat, skunk, possum, and deer,
first people, native dwellers, and the layers on layers of colonists
heaped on the pine-rich soil,
and the billions of things living in that soil,
this is Oakland, this is Oakland,

not some deed pissed in a corner,
not some condo block crushing the earth,
but the life and folk made of that land, the land that Oakland owns.
There is a deep tremor forming, a trembling fissure
wrought by Oakland of itself, a geologic
certainty of rock and bone and mind
that comes to cleanse the land again of all
delusion, of all who grab, who imagine they possess,
who imagine grip and sale and claim.
That comes to shake. That comes to raze.
Hold tight, my sisters, my brothers, my humans
whom I call *my* out of mere affection,
out of empathy and welcome and the urge to well,
let us learn to ride ripples with fastidious soles,
let us learn to not own,
let us learn to dwell and fiercely dwell
and let the owners rip themselves to shreds
as they eat themselves from the inside out,
while we drink sky and mind and nourish
from the milk of each other's hearts,
churning a new species who will walk through walls.

HAIKU

Gunshots in the city night
stir me from my sleep,
my brain on auto-prayer.

BROKEN CITY

The broken city is pretty.
I like the smell of it breaking.
Can I please have a glass of absinthe
with a ball bearing and a dusting of chalk?

EATING AN EGG

Ripped from the womb of an angry bird

you slide down my throat with such ease

I could almost believe myself peaceable.

EARTH PUNK

Call me Earth Punk and step away if you don't. I'm not here for
the fashion. I'm not here for the hair. I'm not here for the scene
or the being seen. I'm here for the passion. I'm here for the song.
I'm here for the truth and noise and anger and politics. I'm here
for the dirt. For digging in dirt. For the politics of dirt. Digging
the loam, the must, the marrow, digging the mirror of the mind,
the unkempt world, digging the space between molecules, the
space between us, the lines and lack of lines, the borderless, the
endless flow and interchange, the pulsing skinless fallacy of I.

I'm here for the digging. I'm here for the roots and air, the
striving outward, the grappling. I'm here for the suck of wind, the
information of sun, for the finding of the dew. I'm here for the
rain. For the sheer cleansing drench of rain. For the pounding
soaking rain that drums away difference, that drains away spite.
That deionizes the sky and land. That deionizes us, turns friction
into grass, melts conflict into luscious soil, feeds life. I'm here for
the taste of it, the taste of earth in my cells, the scent of lightning,
the hair-raising audacity of trees. The resoluteness of trees. Got
conflict? Got oppression? Got strife? Yes! Lie face down between
old roots and take a deep draught. Then decide a course of action.

The politics of earth are no different than the human melee. Yes,
we love each other, and yes, we fuck each other up, always have
and always will just like moon ocean rock leaf ice flame rain dust.
But unlike our muddled monkey-thoughts, the ideology of soil is
relatively pure – live and rot, become, transmit, transform. Sure,
you can cage life, sell the air, pretend to own the sun, rip and tear
and die writhing in inexorable need, or you can be the vine that
twines and stays. Eat dirt, sisterbrothers. Drink sky, my friends.
Wrap yourselves in lakes and stone. These are not commands.
I'm Earth Punk. I don't command. I don't even ask. These are
what you do every day. These are what you are. Dig?

#we

When I wake up queer,
it's like every other day.
Like every day since I came out of my mother.
I don't know what any of this means.
But I do know the rollercoaster,
the ins and outs of light,
the flickering,
the pounding beat,
the omniphonic symphony of cells.
I know my cells, my nerves,
my stink and hair, and I know
that someone called them queer.
Applied the term queer.
Maybe it was me. I. The
phenomenon referenced as I.
Or maybe it was everyone.
In any case, "queer" – a sound
with a history, from the German "quer" –
oblique, cross, adverse, perverse, deviant.
Oblique: slanted or sloping, asymmetrical,
indirect, evasive – I am most of these,
sometimes all when I include the latter two,
when in fact I need to shade my queerness
for the sake of safety, perceived or real.
Cross: I cross streets with my walk,
step after step, breath after breath,
I cross boundaries and proprieties,
word after word, breath after breath,
I cross my own queer shadow indirectly.
Adverse: I oppose intolerance, I face aggression
(or am faced by it), I turn toward ignorance, toward fists,
and I observe them, and sometimes I am afraid,
afraid to move, afraid to stay, but I let them know I am observing,
and I wait to be seen, for eyes to light, and sometimes I am struck.
Perverse: I am turned the wrong way
because somebody made the sound "wrong",
said I am twisted, bent; I turn away from the truly bent

whose nature has been torqued from human back to mammal,
I smell their fear, I turn away, I gather, I turn toward.
Deviant: I take the side roads, the small roads,
I range off-road, into the wilderness, into the wild,
far from nonsensical structures, laws and manners,
into the open space unshadowed by towers and norms
where civility and anarchy meet and caress and fuck.

Now that's queer.

That's queer because it defies the utterance of others, or of
    those who other, and loves the utterance of those who *we*.
That's queer because it takes things as they are, as much as one
    can, it allows where centuries of stone would otherwise
    staunch.
That's queer because it allows, because it lets the vine grow
    wild, the thirsty drink, the body become and behave and
    be a new form, a new shape stretching and writhing in its
    own splendor, its own light, its own scent turning heads
    across the countryside to see what new thing has emerged.
That's queer because it allows the new, damns preconception,
    damns presumption, curses definition for the infinite, lets
    the mind see what it will, not what it wants, not what it
    expects but what it doesn't expect, what might be.
That's queer because it savors when propriety pulls back its chair,
    folds its hands, and watches warily, wantonly, bewitched as
    queerness unfolds itself on the table.
That's queer because it smells good, because it feels right, and
    that's always okay.
That's queer because it has its own scent, knows its own scent,
    because it knows its face, in whatever configuration, of
    whatever kind, kindly and surely, it is what it is.
That's queer because it knows what it is, even when struck.
    Especially when struck.
That's queer because you know what you are, I know what I am,
    we know what we are, because you are what you are, I am
    what I am, we are what we are, because you feel right, I feel
    right, we feel right.

That's queer because it feels right in my bed. It feels particular,
    specific, necessary, whole, ecstatic. Because it belongs. Because
    it feels normal, right, the most normal thing there is, entwined
    and drifting perfectly to sleep.

When I wake up queer, I wake up.
I wake up to normalcy.
I wake up to skin, to touch, to human scent, my own or another's or
    both.
I wake up to easy air. To my lungs accepting air with ease. To
    delicious air. To acceptance.
I wake up to seeing and being seen.
I wake up to all the human shit we pull on each other – longing,
    confusion, presumption, jealousy, sadness, acceptance. Seeing
    and being seen.
I wake up to we, to being one with the species rather than outcast, I
    wake up to connection, to a sense of umbilicus.
I wake up to we, to the many inside me, to they that comprise
    me, to the kaleidoscopic whorl of being and sense and life.
    To the tourbillion of life.
I wake up to we, to the verb of we, to the act of we, *to we* as in *to
    be* as in *to free* as in to accept, to allow, to welcome.
I wake up to welcome, to the elusive welcome of being in the
    world, of moving forward, of inventing new forms of being,
    existence and purpose and joy.
I wake up to the elusive which is not elusive at all, despite what
    they say, because queer is not elusive, queer is here, queer is
    very here, queer is evolving, queer is thriving, queer is we.
Queer is normal because queer is everyone and everything, and
    everyone is queer because there is no normal. Normal is
    ideology. Normal is propaganda. Normal is queer.
Queer is every day, and every day is queer. Every night is queer.
    Every sleep is queer and every waking is queer.

When we wake, we queer. Like every other day.
I don't know what any of this means, because this isn't about
    meaning. It's about being. It's about doing. It's about living.
So let us live, fiercely, softly, colorfully, darkly, queerly, as the
    need requires.

Let us be. Let us very be.

Let us do, and breathe, and do, and touch, and do, and rest, and do, and wake, and do.

Let us queer, as we are, as we can, as we want, as we will, as we must.

Let us we.

PERSONAL GOVERNMENT

For the purposes of national defense
radar waves bombard every inch
pervade every square inch of the landscape
rock tree frog bird fox human landscape:
uuoonnuuoonnuuoonnuuoonnuuoonn
entering every brain jiggling
vibrating every brain cell consistently
calm subtle calm dazedream that's better
than Magic Fingers than instant television:
uuoonnuuoonnuuoonnuuoonnuuoonn forever
graduated intensity education income consistency
o let us harp it's not the sedation
it's the principle
They know They who say *do it* know
no karma will come of it
the outcome will not jut its pallid face
no panic will come of it no snarl
it's the sedation:
uuoonnuuoonnuuoonnuuoonnuuoonn über alles
mama told me not to come mama told me not to come
she said that ain't the way to have fun son
that ain't the way to have a summer vacation
I sat calm on a log above a small pool
in the calm heat in wooded Canada
I did not untie my tennis shoes
I dangled my feet close to the surface
I forgot the radar the harping the sedation
they did not exist
I tapped my foot on the water
the only waves on the water the only waves
everywhere flowed from the tip of my tennis shoe

MILITARY HUSBAND JAW SONNET

I stir my store-bought yogurt
tiredly over the sink,
watching the pre-formed cup-shape
held by the viscous sweet-sour glop
dissolve under the churning steel of the spoon.
It rises first in a peak well past the lip of the cup –
I think of glaciers and glacial ridges –
then plummets backward into cream.
I'm not worried about the possibility
that it could crest the lip and drop,
leaving me with a splattered mess instead of breakfast.
Later in life I drive my beat-up old van
across the beach and into the ocean,
just because I always wondered
what that would feel like.

The ad on my Android reads:
"Military Husband Jaw Dropped
After Seeing Her Transformation".
I pause for a moment over that missing "'s",
wondering whether its absence might be a result of
rushed work, vernacular, or purposeful manipulation,
but I am mostly taken by the photo below
of a well-known Black American actress,
at least well-known by those aware of Black American actresses,
who is also noted for being a proud woman of size.
Beneath her glowing face the ad continues:
"Husband didn't even recognize his wife
after returning from Afghanistan........",
followed by a red "Read the Story" button
and the TIME® Magazine logo without the ®.
Since this woman is not actually a "military wife"
but in fact a gorgeous Black American actress of size,
I wonder what her fictitious husband had supposedly
been doing in Afghanistan, exactly what transformation
had purportedly occurred, and whether that dropped jaw

was meant to be a sign of good or bad things to come.
I don't click on the ad.

Later that day I read that a local sports team
has once again won the championship,
and that cheering crowds have taken to the streets,
overturning cars, smashing store windows, looting
and destroying property, and setting things on fire.
They are presided over by hordes of the local constabulary,
who, coincidentally, just the week before,
had presided over a large protest and street action
involving many of the same residents in much the same location,
at which time they had controlled the crowd with
flash-bangs, tear gas, shields, beatings, and mass arrests.
On this occasion, however, they are hanging back,
and some can even be seen cheering along with the crowd.
It is their team too, after all.
And another car lights up, another car owned
by a struggling working class man who depends on it
to feed his family, a man who might be in that crowd himself.

Just because it gives you a hard on
doesn't mean you should do it.

LICHEN

If lichen were the last thing alive on Earth, as it likely will be, it would no longer be pretty, it would no longer be small, it would no longer be colorful, it would no longer be fascinating. It would be Big King Boss, and it would rule itself into a corner. It would be cannibal and freak, uncompromised opportunist, and god. It would be father-killer and mother-seller, it would change the color of sky, it would crumble every rock to dust. And why not? Everyone gets their chance to destroy the world, and better yet to be creative and amused by it. It's really quite easy. Watch this.

CANNIBALISM

The fact that we are cannibals
doesn't seem to faze us,
as long as we have somebody
to tell us that we're not.
Let's elect someone to do just that.

GO TEAM

Team beat. Yeah! We're number one. Yeah! You're small. Yeah! We're bigger. Yeah! We're the best. Yeah! You're not much. Yeah! We, you. Yeah! We, you. Yeah! We're real. Yeah! You're not. Yeah! We're important. Yeah! You're shit. Yeah! You're other. Yeah! You're other. Yeah! Stay over there. Yeah! Fetch my drink. Yeah! Fetch my car. Yeah! Clean my car. Yeah! Clean my toilet. Yeah! My my. Yeah! Mine mine. Yeah! Not yours. Yeah! You're nothing. Yeah! I own you. Yeah! Die in pain. Yeah! Eat my shit. Yeah! Fuck you. Yeah! Natural order. Yeah! Natural order. Yeah! Team beat. Yeah! We're number one. Yeah!

MAGA POEMS

MAGA Poem #1

The Idea About America

The idea about America
is to make as much money as possible,
as fast as possible,
by doing as little as possible.
That's it.
That's the whole idea.
Everything else is like a side thing.
Everything else just happens.
This is the only thing that happens on purpose.
Everything else is just chum.

MAGA Poem #2

America Is Not For Pussies

America is not for pussies,
though a good piece of pussy is great once in a while.
But that doesn't mean it's FOR them.
It's for hard-dicked, big-balled MEN
who show pussies exactly what's what.
That's who America is for.
We made it, and we're gonna keep it.
Let the pussies have Scandinavia or something.

MAGA Poem #3

Get With The America Program

Get with the America program
if you wanna keep your shit,
if you like seeing your mom and sisters,
if you like being able to step outside.
I'm not talkin about immies,
they don't belong here anyway.
I'm talkin about YOU, buddy.
This is OUR outside,
and if you don't like that
you can get the fuck outta here
or face the consequences.
That's right, you heard me.
This is OUR America.
I'm talkin about AMERICA.

MAGA Poem #4

The Immies and the Gimmes

They all want something.
That's all they do is want things.
They don't work, they don't even wash,
they just steal, and rape, and kill,
and sit around eating our food and fucking shit up.
Those immies need to get the fuck outta here
and back to the shithole countries they came from.
And the gimmes, who cares if they was born here,
we should throw them into one a those shithole countries too.
Nobody gets a free ride in America.
I would puke my beer all over em,
cept it would be a waste of good beer.
Who's buyin?

MAGA Poem #5

God Likes America

If America was on Facebook, God would like us.
How do I know?
Because God likes me, and I'm an American.
I'm one of the good guys.
I know what America is, and I'm gonna keep it that way.
We don't need none of those not American
foods, or cars, or people or anything.
And we sure don't need any of your not American opinions.
Got some? Come over here and tell me.
I'll stab you in the throat.
That's the way God does things,
and that's the way America does things.
God likes America.

MAGA Poem #6

Tell Me About It

Tell me about it. Go on.
Let me hear all a your CNN bullshit
so I can punch you into the next room.
So I can laugh in your face.
Cause that's what you are, laughible.
You yap all about your free speech
but I don't wanna hear it
cause it's not America.
Free speech is only free if it's the right speech.
I'll tell you what.
So the next time you open your mouth
with your free speech, remember that you're wrong first,
and my fist is waiting to tell you that.
Now that's free speech right there.
Tell me about it.

MAGA Poem #7

Don't Gimme That Shit About Racism

Don't gimme that shit about racism,
cause racism isn't real.
I'll tell you about racism.
You know what it's like growin up white in America?
All the races getting everything except the white race,
and we was here first.
Fuck this BLM shit.
All those people are fake Americans anyway,
that's why their lives don't matter,
that's the whole *point*.
We'll get back to the slave thing any minute now,
or send your ass back to Africa.
You'll see what's what.
The natural order is what.
America is what.

MAGA Poem #8

I'll Tell You Why Trump Rules

I'll tell you why Trump rules,
cause he does whatever the fuck he wants
and doesn't give a shit who likes it or not.
Now that's living.
That's what America is supposed to be like,
all the other ways to live are the fake news ways.
Plus he's cleanin the place up real good.
He drained that DC swamp dry, I'll tell you,
there's not a single drop left.
He kicked all those immies right back where they came from,
and kept all their filthy kids to make sure they stay the fuck gone.
He puts all the shitfucks right in their place.
This guy is KING, and King of America,
and we're gonna make damn sure of that,
you better believe it.

MAGA Poem #9

Don't Tell Me What To Do

Don't tell me what to do.
Who the fuck are you anyway?
We got FREEDOM here in America
and that means I'm gonna do
whatever the fuck I want,
just like Trump.
I'm tellin you,
tell me one more time
to wear one of your stupid fake masks
for your stupid fake covid that isn't real anyway
and you're just tryin to give me brain damage,
how stupid do you think I am.
Tell you what,
I'll spit some of that covid right in your face
so you can go die.
Now there's freedom for you.

MAGA Poem #10

Fuck You Go Die

Fuck you go die.
I've been waiting for years to get my hands on you,
and now I can't wait another second,
cause you're the problem with America, Senator.
Your like some kind of cancer.
Take that, bitch. Shut up.
Next time it'll be harder
you baby eating piece of shit.
I'm gonna show you the real America.
Got something else here for you to eat.
Lemme get some a this glock in your mouth,
see how you like the taste a that.
No, not like that, dumbass.
You don't know shit.
Do I have to show you everything?
Watch me. You take it like th———

GLUTEN-FREE BETSY ROSS DOLL

comes at you with a knife, screams,
Gimme sum morra that beer!
and collapses in a sobbing heap.
What is it about America
that makes this all so possible?
She rips her bodice and reveals a huge
Pinocchio tattoo encompassing her breasts.
It was a birthday gift from George, she explains,
seeing your disquietude. *He inked it himself.*
So much for sewing flags and quilting bees; we now
aspire to become America's Top New Genital, while
worker bees and shining geniuses of color are gunned down
in the streets, pureed, and folded into insecticide.
A drone hovers somewhere above you, buzzing, buzzing,
pisses on your head, and Twitters your reaction to the NSA.
Betsy picks herself up slowly, straightens her disheveled everything,
looks down the street and says, *I'm gonna catch the 39*
out to Paradise Point. That's where all the action is.
— and walks away, trailing a musk of longing and despair.
You pick up the knife and lunge at the nearest pedestrian,
a podiatrist in a sandwich board. The knife
sticks in the board between the image of the second and middle toe.
You scream, *Gimme sum morra that beer!*
The podiatrist barks, *Two for a dollar! Two for a dollar!*
and walks on, blade still firmly planted in their signage.
You look wistfully for Betsy, seeking some
sort of connection to the past, but she has been labeled a commodity,
swept up, and sold to a horny vegan tech bro.

WITH NATION, WITH LOVER

Buried in work my mind begins to drift
and thereupon I dream a funny
scrolling sentimental list of
70's TV sitcoms: *Mary Hartman,*
Mary Hartman; *The Courtship of Eddie's*
Father; *Love, American Style*:
and in my goofy sleep I smile
until the list rolls up an odd
title of a show I'd never seen
(in fact was never made) but that I
nonetheless endearingly recalled,
a caterwauling hit about
an ardent President, based
upon a long-lost poem (never
writ) by jubilant Walt Whitman –
a little giggle-hearted farce
about a President who treats
his loving country as if it
(absurdly as it sounds) might be
the one he cares about the most –
imagine that – as if he cared
about the health and wealth of every
citizen as she or he or they
might have a value personally
beyond the mass psychosis, cash –
as if he really gave a shit
about a single form of life
beyond that motherless mutation,
corporation, Darwin's doll –
as if he recognized as kin
all the people living here,
fought the stark dehumanizing
forces of the popular,
and strove to be, as Whitman saw
(or might have seen), *With Nation, With Lover.*
What a show that must have been.

NOTICE BE PROVIDED

The authority for collecting the requested information
participation in the
Program
is voluntary
but the requested information is necessary for participation.

Principal purpose
identity
eligibility and benefits
to permit the servicing
to locate you and collect.

Routine uses
disclosure to agencies
private parties
guaranty agencies
credit bureau
educational and financial.

Contractors
verify your identity
eligibility and benefits
servicing
repayment efforts
possible fraud
verify compliance
or to locate you.

Information
may be disclosed.

Third parties
authorized to assist in administering.

Private firms
processing and analyzing
maintain safeguards.

Federal agencies
computer matching programs for the verification of information
eligibility for benefit
debt collection
prevention of fraud, waste, and abuse.

You must provide all.

Requires that when any
requests that you disclose
be advised
mandatory or voluntary
what statutory
and what uses.

Disclosure
required to participate
consistently requires the disclosure.

Forms and documents
adopted pursuant.

Your SSN
your identity
an account number
throughout the life
to record necessary data accurately.

An identifier
used in
eligibility
status
deferment
cancellation
tracing and collecting
you become delinquent
you default.

SONNET ON THE ORIGINS OF WRITTEN LANGUAGE IN MESOPOTAMIAN CULTURE AS AN ESOTERIC TOOL FOR CROWD CONTROL

The first tribal cultures had an organic
power structure; one did whatever one could.
With the dawn of stable cultures, cities grew,
men of power-lust were faced with the trick
of transubstantiating themselves, random
as asses, to shepherd over the lowing throng.
Simple solution: they plucked the mounting fear
of mortality, rife in the growing mind, to wield
a phantom message from the Great Beyond.
They carved a daunting pedestal inscribed
with blah blah blah blah, first unforeseen code
until the code was cracked, the pedestal cracked
into terrible words: "You can possess the lives
of men obsessed with that which they cannot
possess. Make a wanton mystery of death."
Alas, only a few have learned to read.
Subvert the mystery, the stark banal
subversion of all our clarity.

SANCTITY

Cartographers around the world
muster glances at the markless map.
So unmolested, so sensuous, it rides upon them
as a white steed on glass.
Beneath their shattered shacks the live plain roars,
reaping and eking a hungry age
brimming with antelopes, wheat, white-breasted cormorants
diving for prey, tundra, rhizomes, ramifying oaks,
young dogs nipping, cantaloupes bursting, marrow, shale,
vast fields of daffodils, listening mares, sandstorms,
mollusks tossed by the tide, billions of flora in the gut,
lizards, viruses, pith, dew, urgent gnats, cracked worlds,
and addled sapiens flailing about
gorging on pride, lines, pales, accounts, triple-damned marks,
sense of scent plugged by the compulsive mind,
ripp'd from their follicles stinking of earth,
smelling only the ink in their fear-shifted hearts,
the madness that stamps maps with blood.

INTENTION

If we could live in
times of clear ascent,
in a land purged of
boors and miscreants, all
sent to tiny rooms
to ravel string, our
story would be one
of absolute catastrophe,
easily among the most
earnest misendeavors of the
nurturing world, who herself makes
people bent and torn
and feeds them anyway.
Of all the cruel
and misspent ideologies that splay the
canvas of all living things, our ethical
props that purvey sanctimonious
lessons of progress dwell most in that
never-never land of
nod where all great and well-intentioned
actions lead without fail to a
you that cannot fail, a phantasm
of grace
whose mind admits a
catatonia, hungry and void
of sense, that steals
your riveting face.

UNCERTAIN

There may or may not be a sun. Okay. What are you worried about? You still have your Cheerios in a bowl. You still get to root for your sports team. You still want that really nice car. Life goes on, and there's a song in your ear, a cat crossing the street. It looks like rain. The sky is dark today. Of course there's a sun, you say. Of course these are my shoes. Of course that guy glared at me. I don't have time for this. Get outta my face.

~ ~ ~

I make sounds and I think I've said something. You hear sounds and your hand moves. Your scalp moves. We came out of our mothers. Fuck, what a scene. What a noise that must have been. What a smell. Fecal and bloody. Digestive. We eat other living things. We force them inside of us. You call that fair? You call that? What sounds they made. They were born too, if that's how you wanna say it. Carried. Spurted forth. Dirt in all of us. Came out wet from our mothers. Stinking. We make sounds. We think we know things.

~ ~ ~

You know me, I just... Well you do know me, don't you? Wait, what? Why would you say that? I'm not like that at all! Why would you even think that? Don't assume on me. You don't like it when people assume shit about you, do you? I know it happens all the time, but does that make it okay to perpetuate the cycle? No, it's not harmless. I couldn't agree less. It's a microaggression, it's water dripping on your head, it's a trickle of violence that makes way for a runnel that makes way for a river. You can think what you want about that, or about me. It's not my job to change the way you think. Just don't for a moment imagine that you know me. You don't. You don't fucking know me.

LET'S PRETEND

Is every landlord evil? Is every Capitalist insane? Do we need to eat cupcakes with Karl Marx in order to even discuss this? Let's pretend there's a giant bunny in the room, and talk about it until everybody believes it's there. Why? So that they'll give us their cupcakes. It'll be fun. It'll be just between us. Let's pretend there's a room. Let's pretend there's a table. Let's pretend there are cupcakes. Let's pretend there's a giant syndicalist system that works for everybody, in which no one ever becomes corrupt. Let's pretend there's free trade. Let's pretend there's truth. Let's pretend prosperity comes to those who work. Let's pretend everyone has an equal chance. Let's pretend you have an equal chance. Let's pretend there's you.

LAMENT

Abundant are the ways of men,
oft shorn or shearing by the self-sure eye
that ratifies the charnels we abide
and come to bide in us.
What slithered into fetal you,
perhaps defenseless zygote,
promulgating the inchoate I?
What hirsute drive became the flaming spire?
The painful vowel transpires us into
the reed-wracked, steel-stacked shacks
we so admire, while flailing and discrete
we shit ourselves atop the pile, piercing spleens
and brows indiscriminately, rending wombs with shanks
of pride or infants with the death-struck mind.
What slithered in or nested there both loves and fears
the apparent skin, and ape-like shapes
itself to emulate the impenetrable,
worshipping the rat-trap rage,
brutality of the ivory tower,
rape of fleeting forms for the sad
illusive sense of mass,
and a wall like an eyelid.
Who are you is the fucked up
question of our mortal need,
suckling monsters greedy for the crown
and substantiation of a seamless room.
And we are left with damage marrow-deep
shuddering its way through transigent flesh
and into the saturated heart of world, the unclept next,
and generations cast upon the road.
Severed, torn, we catalyze the load.
The daughters who were fucked
have not washed, the daughters
who were fucked have not washed,
the daughters who were fucked
have not washed.

43

BANG BANG

What is all this banging – the banging we call America? Is it a million hammers, some might hope, a million guns exploding in the chest, our ever-cracking foundations of integrity, or the nail of education driven through the skull between the eyes? Holy shit, what a bluster. And all we can say is *Let's fix it*? That's like asking any politician not to lie, like asking any CEO to care who dies. A giant joke! Yes, I'm in a mood – the mood of watching the streets stream with the blood of the manipulated. We don't need a fix, sisters, brothers, we have our fix, this is a fix. Don't kid yourself, your cries fall on no ears at all – they're off laughing in their vichyssoise. They won't relent, and they sure as hell won't be stopped by the arms or books of justice. They'll grind and grind until we've no throats left to cry. So enough with the crying. Show them some cold hard finely hammered steel. Bring back the guillotine, I say. Just set it out on the National Mall. Let's see what the sight of that does to their potato soup.

AHH, AMERICA,

what a beautiful blade you have hidden under your gown. I'd like to see you use it. Oh wait, you just did. What moves. What panache. I love seeing you in action, America, because it shows me what we are, the mystery of us revealed. What beauty you are. What teeth. You're such an animal. You're such a dance. You're such a leading-into-fire. Such blood. Pungent and thick. No wonder we're so turned on.

A FABLE

One day when the prime lending rate jumped thirty percent, unexpectedly and without precedent, all the capitalists in the world began to float. These were no bush-league capitalists, however, not mere consumers or dabblers in the game, but the true die-hard believers who had planted capitalism like a compressed air valve deep in their vacuous hearts. Slowly they rose at first, just a few inches or feet, buoyed by the market rate like ducks in a lake, like gnats in an updraft, though by evening their levitation had brought them all, a good 16.7% of the population, somewhere about ten feet above ground level. Everyone seemed to notice but they, who went about their business and bobbed home for the night as if nothing out of the ordinary had happened. So it went for a week or so, when the mortgage rate shot up and so did they accordingly, another fifty feet or so. Still they kept their blue teeth charged and had sundries and luxuries delivered by an army of drones. After that is was the NASDAQ, pushing them to about three hundred, then inflation, then income taxes for everyone but them. People began to suspect a collusion, though after a month or so the capitalists settled at about a mile up, and it was difficult to reach them for comment (let alone see them). Planes were rerouted and satellites kept track. Meanwhile the economic situation below became more and more desperate. Prices had risen so high and wages so low that people were actually accepting pay to dig their own graves. Everyone scrambled for a buck, a bird, and a TV set. Mob-robs and loot-fests became the daily news. Then finally it happened. People just stopped buying things. Initially most folks simply took what they needed, and nobody around them cared. They took, and cheered, or abstained, and starved. Millions died. Still there was less and less to take, and less and less to take from. So they started making things and trading for what they needed. They had no choice – money was just no good any more. They began to barter, and in what seemed like days, a whole new system sprang up, frugal but vibrant. Soon they forgot the capitalists existed, and began to till what was left of the blighted land. A hard road, a teeth-gritting road with small fulfillments sprout by stingy sprout, scant but no other road there was. Then came the first thud, then another and another. Capitalists were falling from the sky. Many wailed, threw up their arms in horror and dismay. But only briefly, for they soon realized what the fallen capitalists were good for, and set about to fertilize the earth.

O CORPORATION, YOU ARE NOT IMMORTAL

O plug the merry plug, you tedious
face of death, you impossible freak,
plug the silky siren in and shunt
the silence of its saccharine song
into the linty bureau of your splintering,
rapt, rapacious heart—O eat
the plucky mare, the tedious mace,
the mass of death, O eat and eat
the sabine heat, the chattering flock,
the ambitious dull, O eat and plug and stuff
the flinty sorrow of the captive mind
into the rancid love boat of your hacking
want, your flatulent eye—O stuff,
and eat, and plug, and hack, hack away
hewing freak, hawing cancer, hiving horse,
howling mentor, cannibal drunk, hypnotist
of the mewling spree, chimera, canker,
soft dis-ease, hackneyed genius of a
volute sense, tyrannic enzyme, flawed macaw,
sanctum, slaughterhouse, verdant scree,
mother of nihil, father of a twisted tongue,
myopic utopia, dementia unbound—
eat it all up, yes, like a good bunny
—chow down, fucker, stuff it down,
stuff it all the way, plug it in, clamp down,
and gloat—chew your cheeks, pucker up,
like a champing Jesus gloat, har the hardy har
and plug all the stops, plug every pore—
Leak not, O Corporation—and bloat,
bloat huge, bloat baleful, bloat bilious,
bloat immobile and freeze, blackheart,
from the bunions up—freeze a roiling
babble stew, freeze a sphincterous clench,
freeze basaltic, freeze stench to dust,
freeze breath, freeze nerves, freeze face,
freeze in mid-gaw, freeze the minions of your
tantric tongue to autonomic blades, freeze

that tantalizing rictus of your cawing maw,
and hack—hack above all, hack
blood to boil, joints to rust, hack
egregious rhetoric to pandering excuse,
hack the corpses from your safe,
hack the vital organs loose,
hack vision to a dwindling speck,
hack all your being to a desiccating sty,
and die, and die, and die.

Shapiro, Irving. *The New Dictionary of Legal Terms*. Flushing, NY: Looseleaf Law Publications, 1984.

From: "CORPORATE PERSONALITY"

The distinct status of a business organization that has complied with law for its recognition as a legal entity that has an independent legal existence from that of its shareholders.

The Encyclopedia Americana. Danbury, CT: Grolier, 2000.

From: "CORPORATION"

A classic expression of the sovereignty doctrine is the opinion of Chief Justice John Marshall in the Dartmouth College case in 1819: "A corporation is an artificial being, invisible, intangible, and existing only in contemplation of the law. Being a mere creature of law, it possesses only those properties which the charter of its creation confers upon it either expressly or as incidental to its very existence. These are such as are supposed best calculated to affect the object for which it was created. Among the more important are immortality, and, if the expression may be allowed, individuality; properties by which a perpetual succession of many persons are considered as the same, and may act as a single individual. They enable a corporation to manage its own affairs, and to hold property without the perplexing intricacies, the hazardous and endless necessity, of perpetual conveyances for the purpose of transmitting it from hand to hand."

THE PATH HOME

Wild eye caught the wave, is swimming in shoes, microwaves, cars, pavilions, scars. Ain't nuthin better than a fast-track train to fortune, until a jet engine lands in your lap and you soar. It's all about the flash, baby, all about the shine – your time is fly, is flying, is flashing by and all you need is everything, earth and sky and in-between. And why? Because we said so, because the flow is steady, the green is ready and you take take take it fuck me yeah. Wild eye caught the fly, caught the net, bet your life and warped the weft and look what's left – chunks of flesh in a pile, miles of arms, two billion breaths and gasping, gasping, where's the subway, where's the car, how did we get here, how far to home, is it still there, what do we own, how many parsnips, how many nails, how many pieces of you left drowning in a sea of rails.

SHRUG

We're all material girls in our sepulcher-mall of a world. So pile
thy barrow! A wardrobe upon you! Soundwaves upon you!
Comforts upon you! Pushcarts upon you! Bedding upon you!
Wine-racks upon you, beer chests and full-stocked bars!
Jewelry upon you, tons of it! Chain-link upon you! SUV's upon
you! Truckloads of chocolate and salt upon you! Suitcoats upon
you! Hot mud upon you! Houses upon you! Rationales upon
you! Resumes upon you! All the shoes in the world upon you!
Applause and degrees upon you! Pedigrees upon you!
Hierarchies upon you! Statuary upon you! Relentless deafening
mangling remote-controlled mind-traps upon you in skyward
heaps! And atop all an intractable sludge of asphalt paving the
best and newest city built just for you with everything you
could ever want that will last forever. Shrug that shit off.

JANUS

The great head turns, dripping hair in unnatural runnels that reveal, as it revolves, a second face, planted firmly where the skull-butt should reside. It gapes its mouth, attempts to speak, but only a foul breath erupts. It is a wind rank with corruption, with bursting cells and organs of its once sweet flesh. The turn continues, and we cheer to see the other face and so be rid of this one. It must be safer, prettier, less dire. But as it comes to view, we see that it is not, rather one of insatiable glittering eyes maddened by status, and great white razored teeth with chunks of dead and stinking mammal lodged between. This face roars, a roar that becomes a lengthy laugh, tumultuous chuckle trampling you in its force. You pick yourself up, and wonder which to join, as if by habit or instinct you have to take a side. The foul-breathed face is coming round again, this time with a crooked grin. Which will you choose? Can you choose both? Or will you go walking through a field, down to a small stream, to listen to the water words?

LOOK

Some people look at each other and some people don't. What does that mean? I'll let you decide. In the meantime, I'm looking at you, I'm looking at you for no other reason than curiosity, commonality, and the tide. I am compelled, I am compelled and others are not, so it seems or maybe I'm wrong but I'm compelled and I know why, not yours to say, not yours to guess just my eye, just my why, mine. And maybe yours, maybe your why, maybe our why, look at us looking, look at us ducking, look at us staring at the wall. Look at us stare in the mirror, look at us bear too much gaze, look at us fare alone or together, some people look and some people don't.

ASSUME THIS

Assume it's raining. Assume you're in a good mood. Assume that's because it's raining. Assume the air is clean. Assume it isn't. Assume the kitchen is a healthy place. Assume your parents were right. Assume you're right too. Assume you'll go out today. Assume you won't wear a hat. Assume your head will get completely drenched. Assume you'll walk down the street. Assume you want some coffee. Assume you meet the love of your life. Assume neither of you has the wherewithal to notice. Assume you go on with your life. Assume things are good. Assume the rain stops, and the grass is very green, saturated. Assume a car drives over the curb and skids through the grass. Assume some of the grass is crushed and dying. Assume some of it will grow back. Assume you're crushed and dying. Assume none of you will grow back. Assume a man comes over and stands looking down at you. Assume that man is I. Assume I calmly, almost serenely tell you this entire story. Assume I'm lying.

~ ~ ~

You're called in to your boss' office and assume that you're about to be fired, though you have no idea why. Maybe it's because you don't dress right. Maybe it's because you were rude to that customer, though in all fairness they were rude first. Maybe you just don't look right. You step in. Your boss is shuffling papers and says, without looking up, "Take a seat." You do. "I'll be just a minute," he says. You look around. Everything seems spotless and orderly. Those books. Those framed pictures. That perfect plant. Even the paper shuffling sounds orderly. *Rap, rap, rap!* he cracks the stack of papers into alignment, and sets it down with a snap. Folds his hands on the desk and looks across at you. Smiles a big ferocious smile. Here it comes. "You've been here how long?" he asks, grinning and trying to read the shadows behind you. "Two months," you say. "Two months!" he almost chortles. "Has it been that long? Seems like you've only been here a few days..." *So that's his tack,* you posit. His grin gets bigger, toothy, lion-like. "How would you like a raise?" he asks. "A...raise?" you echo dumbly. "Yes," he says, drawing in closer, eyes gleaming, "because you're just so fucking cute."

~ ~ ~

You're at a party. You're not liking the music. The food is kind of strange. You're pretty sure the host has bad politics. You're pretty sure they're racist. You don't know them, but your friend does. Your friend says they're terrific once you get to know them. They have a large iguana in a small tank with a couple of sticks and leaves. It looks depressed. You wonder if iguanas can experience depression. They have nervous systems, don't they? Lymph nodes and hormones? You're not quite sure. Your friend starts talking about snakes. They seem to know a thing or two about them. They say there's no way that snakes perceive the world anything like we do. You say, no way? They have brains, they have eyes, light comes in, they sense danger. It's all instinctual, your friend says. You have to wonder. You once saw a snake eating another snake. That was also in a glass tank. The less fortunate of the two, slimmer, maybe a foot long, was being consumed tail first. About a third of it was inside the larger snake, being crushed and digested, and the rest, right up to its head, stuck out from the mouth absolutely straight and rigid as a pencil, its own mouth opened wide. You'd never imagined seeing a snake straight and rigid as a pencil. You turn to your friend and say, We're all instinctual, then open the top of the iguana's tank, lift it out gingerly, and walk out the front door.

~ ~ ~

You see a person standing on a corner staring at their phone. Are they going to cross the street? Someone is walking toward you up the block. You sense that they're in a bad mood. Is that true? An old woman stands on a lawn looking up at the sky. What is she looking at? Is she looking at anything? Is she okay? Does she need help? You see a mom smack her child, who starts to bawl. You see a man asleep on a bench. You see a small dog walking down the street alone. You see a bicycle lying in the street. Who left it there? Why? You see a wrench on the sidewalk. The words "YOU ARE HERE" scrawled in the cement. A stray seashell. A single shoe. You go into a pharmacy to buy some chocolate, and the cashier is crying, clearly, quietly. You smile at them. You see that same woman on the corner, no longer with phone, staring ahead and crying. The woman on the lawn is also crying. A truck rumbles by, startling you. You look around. Take a slow breath. What are you assuming?

PALATABLE DEPICTION

I see the film.
It comes through my screen.
Another African conflict. Guns. Running.
Maybe the same conflict as the last one.
Ooo, there's some blood. Jeeps.
There's that music, that syncopation,
telling me where I am.
I have to be spoonfed, carefully.
Because I'm American.
Placation nuanced as danger.
There it is, the Africa I know.
Those colors. That sky.
Certain kinds of motion exist there.
Certain wind. Movements. Always danger.
Always bright, a lot of sun,
like the negation of a dark continent.
A negation. A seizure. A crypt,
safe and warm, in which plays a warning
like a familiar syncopation.
Familiar, but not too familiar.
Because I'm American.
Because I am hungry.
I am comfortable.
I know how to read this.
Those brown people are in trouble.
But wait! They've got help,
some white guys with American accents.
They're supposed to be from Israel,
but we know better.
One of them is even a superhero,
so we know everything will turn out okay,
even if it doesn't.
Why else would the film even be here
coming through my screen.
Speeding jeep roars. Those guns are loud.
He saves the little kid.
Yep, this film's for me, all right.

Because I would do the same thing.
I'm hungry.
Hungry for the life I know I could have.
Look at those pecs. That chin.
Those brown people have a lot of scars
and not much agency.
But here's where things get interesting –
the American-speaking white Israeli superhero
is about to come up with a plan, a brilliant plan
that, while not giving the brown people any agency,
will use his agency to help help help them,
because that just the kind of guy I am,
and sure there will be danger (especially for the brown people),
and close calls (especially for the brown people),
and many good people might die (especially the brown ones),
but there will also be bonding and ethical discussions and
      setbacks
and disagreements and interpersonal tensions and maybe even a
      sacrifice
especially amongst the very attractive white international team
      members
that he will put together in an upbeat montage with jazzy music,
each with their specialties, and quirks, and hairdos
that almost make them characters, or characters enough
especially compared to the one main brown character (excluding
      cameos and the 2-D genocidal military villain
      with the huge creepy grin)
who has the biggest scar and leads the hundreds of nameless
      brown non-characters
through danger but not out of danger, in this film though not
      quite helpless
he is also not quite the help but somewhere between helped and
      helping,
whose entire function is to point those betrodden hundreds
      toward the help
(his pointing, that pointed finger his one feint toward agency,
      just as
his nameless followers are not quite helpless because they have
      not yet died),

toward the help he points, toward the pectoral-bearing
    Americanish superhero
with the brilliant crazy plan, a never-been-tried theatrical
    spycraft endeavor
that he's sure will work, he's 99.9% based-on-a-true-story certain
that it will all work out for most everyone, and here he is,
just in the nick of time, coming up with that plan
just as the hundreds of brown people are starting to die
of thirst, and starvation, and bullets, and rapes, and suicides
but not for much longer, no sir, you can see it in his eyes,
thank god for those blue eyes – but wait! –
oh shit! – he's suddenly killed, that wasn't supposed to happen,
a stray bullet from an unknown and unseen character takes him
    right the fuck out
not much use now is he, bunch of meat in the dirt,
looks like that brilliant plan won't be happening any time soon,
and the brown people and their big-scarred leader all turn into
    birds, all kinds of birds, and fly off,
they're taking their true shapes now and soar into the bright
    African sky,
flocking and wheeling, some tearing off solo, some toward the
    trees,
some toward the coast, some to the military camp, some toward
    who knows where...

DIRECTOR'S CUT – ALTERNATE ENDING

[SCENE FADES IN]   ... and here he is,
just in the nick of time, coming up with that plan
just as the hundreds of brown people are starting to die
of thirst, and starvation, and bullets, and rapes, and suicides
but not for much longer, no sir, you can see it in his eyes,
thank god for those blue eyes – but wait! –
oh shit! – he's suddenly killed, that wasn't supposed to happen,
a stray bullet from an unknown and unseen character takes him
    right the fuck out
not much use now is he, bunch of meat in the dirt,
looks like that brilliant plan won't be happening any time soon,

and the brown people and their big-scarred leader all turn into
    birds, all kinds of birds, and fly off,
they're taking their true shapes now and soar into the bright
    African sky,
flocking and wheeling, some tearing off solo, some toward the
    trees,
some toward the coast, some to the military camp, some toward
    who knows where...
and wow, what the fuck just happened, I didn't see that coming,
just when it seemed so well constructed it turns out to be some
    kind of message movie
concocted by those clever Hollywood minds, even though the film
    is only
seventeen minutes long and I'm still hungry.

BONUS FEATURE – ALTERNATE ENDING 2 (STUDIO
    VERSION)

[SCENE FADES IN]   ... but wait! –
oh shit! – he's suddenly killed, that wasn't supposed to happen,
a stray bullet from an unknown and unseen character takes him
    right the fuck out
not much use now is he, bunch of meat in the dirt,
looks like that brilliant plan won't be happening any time soon,
and the brown people and their big-scarred leader all turn into
    birds and fly off,
they're taking their true shapes now and soar into the bright
    African sky
singing in multiple harmonies about lions and pudding,
dancing in the air as all the other animals sing and dance below...
wow, I didn't see that coming, just when it seemed so well
    constructed,
just for me, it turns out to be some kind of feel-good movie
concocted by those clever Hollywood minds, even though the film
    is only
seventeen minutes long and I'm still hungry.

TALKING TO MYSELF WITH NO PANTS ON

Nose-fucked in a garage again and I can't find my hand in the
crashing down, crashing glass in the where's my face again, walls
again, where's the door in the noxious blaze again, one more day
and one more gonna need another lung in the smashing dust –
blow, nay – shun every rock every face every form of spring –
yah, crack – tooth in the febrile jaw in the rash of rectitude, hear
me shriek my name in the dark here I am again, not particularly
comforted, not particularly am again in the room in the shed
fucked in the neck in the year-long bedlam mayhem – hey! mine
– hey! – say – hey! cause whatcha gonna whatcha gonna peace
out on shit in the corner balls in the gutter where's the window I
gotta get out and jump motherfucker face in the smash wall crass
in the kitchen crease in the mirror naked naked naked naked stab
the endless window gathering gathering gathering

THE VIEW FROM MY APARTMENT

I look out my window at the sad world, and realize that it's not sad at all. I am. People are. But the world is not. This is something that I learn every day, and forget every day. It's all part of the story that we tell ourselves over and over in our sleep. It's the story of how sadness fell in love with the world, and what happened next. Of how all the trees lost their leaves one day, and the world shrugged it off, while sadness spent all winter knitting them scarves. Of how we forget again and again because we aren't real, we are the dream, we fade. And of who comes along and falls in love with the dream. And what happens next.

~ ~ ~

I look at my screen and the pixels become needles that slash through my retinas with animate force. Inside my brain they build a new colony of glasslike obelisks in a prismatic maze. I stagger through, daggered and sliced until I find a cold cement corner to rest in. I curl up there shivering until the disorientation settles and I become comfortable. Now I feel ready for anything. I climb the sleek razors out from the screen, and look at the world that's always held danger and salvos and glee, even as primordial seas indifferently bash cliffs to clay, or are they indifferent, are they any different than the hawking legions stampeding their screens with fear of the flesh sharpening them into blades?

~ ~ ~

I look at the news and see Capitalism eating itself from the inside, preparing to sacrifice humanity to save its cankered hide. The opening credits of Metropolis roll, as the bunkered wealthy gorged on ecstasy and brie barter slaves' survival for their roast pork. Armies march down our streets shooting everyone for fun. I learn that there's no immunity to bullets. The song of power-saws whirring everywhere melds in my dreams with crashing cars and the roar of whole cities on fire. I wake to find I haven't woken. I sleep hungry and waiting for the tanks to deliver old bread and momentary stimulus. After that I lie back down in the dark, unsure whether my labored breathing is the result of panic or a virus the size of a fat politician sitting on my chest. I grab my phone, see it still has 17%, and wonder if I should reach out to someone. Instead I look at the news.

~ ~ ~

I look in the mirror and see the eyes I've always had, same eyes, same size, maybe a little more blurry and bloodshot. But mine, whatever that means. I see my face, whatever that means, maybe the face that others see and maybe not, who can tell. I suspect that the mirror holds my face at every age, and I see them all at once, unable to separate the stony edifice that the flower lady sees, or the one that the checkout guy sees, or all the infinite others. And I see my infinity beyond skin, the spaceless force that lives us all, all at once and endless as the duck's eye of eternity. Of course we are inside each other, please don't be afraid, as the rain falls and the roots drink I rejoice from stem and leaf, for we are all wonder, we are all embraced, we are all of every age, into the grave, into the soil, into the flesh, into our ancestors sailing like samaras into the wind, into the solar stream.

I SPY A TWO-PACK OF CONDOMS

I spy a two-pack of condoms that's been dropped on the floor in the waiting area for Gate 45, SFO, and I think, *That loss could change the course of history.* I think, *That could be a matter of life and death, of life, or of death, or of nonexistence.* It's 10:30 in the morning but I got up at 6 so I'm coffeed and bleary and lugging too much shit, and this feels pretty damn early for an existential dilemma, hypothetical or not – or maybe it's in fact the perfect time, since I'm about to fly across North America in 2018 to spend a couple of weeks alone in Mom's big old house in Cape May, New Jersey, on a tiny sand peninsula jutting between the Delaware Bay and the Atlantic Ocean, then a couple of weeks visiting friends in NYC amidst too too too many people, then a ways upstate amidst little towns and never ever enough woodland. I'm looking at a good chunk of time chilling and reflecting and writing and catching some East Coast air and some early spring mid-Atlantic weather, then cavorting and converging and creating and re-creating with people who have known me well for decades, who in some ways are the source and core of my humanness, so in effect I'll be viewing and re-viewing my life to date at a time when I'm definitely muddling through the confusion and muck of my memory and experience, whatever that means, to evaluate whether any of this fits together, whether I've accomplished anything real, whether all this toil, this roil, all these days and all these breaths have been worthwhile. Whatever that means. I look around at the billions of people filtering through this gate, through this causeway, through this terminal to fling themselves into air, or having been flung from melee to melee, throng to throng, culture to culture, kindness to kindness, beauty to beauty, hope to hope, struggle to struggle, strife to strife, conflict to conflict, conflagration to conflagration till all this flinging seems frantic, febrile, forsaken. So I look again at those condoms, and I think, *Yep, those are condoms,* and I think, *Somebody might not get to use them,* and I think, *Somebody might.* Then I don't think for a few moments, nothing at all, thank god for that, and I perk up, I lighten, I feel like something shifted, hit the reset button, and I think, *Anything can happen,* and that's true, anything can, someone will love and someone will die, and every day someone is born who doesn't hate, and who might not grow up hating, and who might say something to make someone else not hate, or stop hating, or never hate, and they might say something too, and so on and so on as we inch toward intelligence, toward compassion, toward humanity, and who cares if this is unknowable, unpredictable, unfashionable, it sounds good to me.

Prescription

I
WANT
TWO
HUNDRED
HANDS
TO
TOUCH
EACH
OTHER
WITH
OUT
RE
GARD
TO
WHOSE
THOSE
HANDS
MIGHT
BE.

NEW PLEDGE

I pledge allegiance to the mind
of the united seers of wilderness.
And to the psychosis we've left behind,
I say,
You are fear.
You are useless.
Evaporate, once and for all.

WE SING AND RISE

text from an installation in a reading space

rise tide sister into shimmer field
embrace sacrum language or risk rift
breathe now and stride

rise fire brother with filament matrix
bring blossoms but shout fracas vibe
study can revive sanity

rise earth animal for intricate time
drum conflict reveal if ardent strive
watch nerve crisis signs

rise living sentinel of care harbor
simmer sentient egg conundrum and celebrate
lift eye to nest

rise breeze winding through sense canyon
release need tensions when will powers
form new culture junction

SPRING SONG

Every time water goes down my throat,
the spring and latch of illusion disappear
and all my senses open for an instant,
crying, Yes, there is light, and sand, lungs, hair,
and the crushed leaves that are my throat
sing the chlorophyll of time, the luscious
shriek, the lull of bark, the pending
tock, the cellular alarum that rips
each breath into a streaming sheen,
a succulent degree of fine
that matters not the cataclysm,
worries not the strife, the wrenching shit,
the falling brick, the rank, the clock,
the thudding shrill and fetid heart
trammeled by stain and fame and utter shorn
delusion of the sick, insistent, dank,
commissioned, calculated void.

Tonight I heard the first catfuck of the season,
and I knew everything would be okay.

Richard Loranger is a writer, performer, musician, visual artist, and all-around squeaky wheel, who has been working around the United States for over forty years. He has lived in many parts of the country, including New York, Austin, Boulder, Chicago, and San Francisco, and he currently lives and works in Oakland, CA.

He is the author of *Unit of Agency, Be a Bough Tit, Sudden Windows, Poems for Teeth, The Orange Book* and ten chapbooks, including *6 Questions* and *Hello Poems*. As well he has had work included in over one hundred magazines and journals and thirty anthologies.

In addition to publications, he has done over 500 featured readings, in venues ranging from Lollapalooza to Intersection for the Arts, City Lights, Paradise Lounge, and Café Babar in San Francisco to The Poetry Project at St. Mark's Church, The Bowery Poetry Club, and Teachers and Writers in New York. He has also been a member of several music and performance groups, including Conspiracy of Beards and The High Risk Group in San Francisco and Performance Art Church in Austin and New York.

In Oakland, he is the founder of Poetea, a monthly literary conversation group. Before the pandemic, he curated a bi-monthly talk and reading series exploring queer perspectives, titled *#we*, and co-curated a quarterly series called Babar in Exile. He hopes to return to hosting and curating sometime soon.

He finds it increasingly challenging to be a mindful provocateur in this day and age. You can find more about his work and scandals at www.richardloranger.com.

BONUS TRACK

Scan here to see
Richard Loranger reading
"O Corporation, You Are Not Immortal",
"DIY",
and a special bonus track.

THESE PIECES HAVE BEEN PREVIOUSLY PUBLISHED

"DIY" in *Correspondence #3* (Brooklyn, NY), March 2010.

"We Have to Become Human" in *october babies* (online journal), January 2010.

"remember:" in *Poetry Expressed* (Berkeley, CA), vol. 2, Spring 2017.

"The Oakland Sky" in *Nomadic Journal: Wonder* (Oakland, CA), September 2018.

"Broken City" in *Escape Wheel*, an anthology of poetry and prose, great weather for MEDIA press (New York, NY), August 2020.

"Earth Punk" in *riverbabble 33* (Oakland, CA), Summer 2018.

"Military Husband Jaw Sonnet" in *Oakland Review #2* (Oakland, CA), October 2015.

"Cannibalism" in *Naked Bulb Summer 2016 Anthology*, Naked Bulb Press (Oakland, CA), April 2017.

"Gluten-Free Betsy Ross Doll" in *Maintenant 14* (New York NY), June 2020.

"NOTICE BE PROVIDED" in *Long Shot 27* (Hoboken, NJ), April 2004 and *Newark Review Online* (New Jersey institute of Technology), vol. 2, set 3, April 1999.

"Sanctity" in *Bay Area Poets Seasonal Review* (Berkeley, CA), vol. 4, no. 3, Spring 2009.

"Intention" in *Oakland Review #4* (Oakland, CA), February 2017.

"A Fable" in *Maintenant 15* (New York NY), June 2021.

"Bang Bang" in the book *Sudden Windows*, Zeitgeist Press (Berkeley,CA), 2015.

"O Corporation, you are not immortal" in *Overthrowing Capitalism, Volume 2,* The Revolutionary Poets Brigade (San Francisco, CA), October 2015 and *Newark Review Online* (New Jersey institute of Technology), vol. 2, set 3, April 1999.

"New Pledge" in *Babyfish #5* (Detroit, MI), June 1991 and *Propaganda #2* (Boulder, CO), May 1991.

"Spring Song" in *Barrow Street* (New York, NY), Winter 2004.

GREAT BIG THANK YOUS

to PAUL CORMAN-ROBERTS and E. LYNN ALEXANDER, for finding this work worth throwing in the literary hopper, for trusting it with the soul of their endeavor, and for bearing such heartful vision and nrg through dark times; to JASON TALLON, SUSAN PEDRICK, STEVE ARNSTON, MARVIN R. HIEMSTRA, and PETER HARTER for loving eyes and minds; that as well to LONELY CHRISTOPHER, and for the kind read and endless interest and support; to RICH FERGUSON, JAMES CAGNEY, DENA ROD, HILARY BROWN, and JUBA KALAMKA, for generously lending an early look; to those who've seen value in these pieces over the years, including CHRIS FUNKHOUSER, BRUCE ISAACSON, J DESALVO, LEILA RAE, ANDY SUNFROG, JANE ORMEROD, and the folks from great weather for MEDIA, Poetry Express, Naked Bulb, *Maintenant*, and *Correspondence*; and to all those whom I've egregiously overlooked – for each of you I wish the most beautiful glass of water.

IF YOU LIKED THIS WORK, YOU MIGHT ALSO ENJOY
THESE BOOKS BY RICHARD LORANGER.

Each book is very different in tone and style.

You should be able to order copies directly from the author, from
the small presses listed, or, if necessary, from various online
booksellers. You can read about these and earlier titles which are
currently out of print at www.richardloranger.com/books-
chapbooks.

Be a Bough Tit, poetry, 52 pp
Be About It Press (Richmond, CA), 2020
www.beaboutitpress.com

Sudden Windows, flash prose, 100 pp
Zeitgeist Press (Las Vegas, NV), 2016
www.zeitgeist-press.com

6 Questions, six poems responding to artwork, 12 pp
Exot Books (Halcott, NY) 2013
www.exotbooks.bigcartel.com

Poems for Teeth, poetry series with artwork, 224 pp
we press (Simsbury, CT), 2005
www.wepress.org

The Day Was Warm and Blue, poetry series, 28 pp
published by the author, 2002

Hello., poetry series in small book form, 67 pp
the author/we press, 2001/2003

Letters for the End Times

Collapse Press is a small literary publisher specializing in poetry and prose by authors, established and new, whose work addresses the current social atmosphere of a society in turmoil and on the verge of transformation.

Unit of Agency is the inaugural publication from Collapse Press.

Watch for these titles coming soon:

Death Haiku by Missy Church
Find Me in the Iris by E. Lynn Alexander
Nineteenth Street Station by Paul Corman-Roberts
Comics for Collapse, Volume 1

and so much more...

Find us any time at

www.collapsepress.com